Racism

Questions and Feelings About ...

There are millions of people in the world.
Every one of us is different.

Racism

Questions
and Feelings
About ...

W
FRANKLIN WA
LONDON•SYDNE

ita Ganeri

by Ximena Jeria

Franklin Watts
First published in Great Britain in 2018 by The Watts Publishing Group

Editor: Melanie Palmer
Design: Lisa Peacock
Author: Anita Ganeri

ISBN: 978 1 4451 6442 7 (Hbk)
ISBN: 978 1 4451 6443 4 (Pbk)

Printed in China

Franklin Watts
An imprint of
Hachette Children's Group
Part of The Watts Publishing Group
Carmelite House
50 Victoria Embankment
London EC4Y 0DZ

An Hachette UK Company
www.hachette.co.uk

www.franklinwatts.co.uk

We look different. We wear different clothes. We speak different languages. We have different ways of living. We're good at different things.

What makes you different?

Even though we're all different, we're all human beings. We should value and respect everyone for who they are.

We should treat everyone fairly and equally. Everyone should have the chance to live and work together happily and peacefully.

How would you like people to treat you?

Some people do not treat others fairly or equally. They treat them badly because they have different coloured skin, come from different countries, speak differently or wear different clothes.
This is called racism.
It is a kind of bullying.

Racism can mean saying unkind things to people. It can mean calling people names or making fun of the way they speak. It can mean teasing them about the way they look or dress.

How would you feel if someone called you names?

Racism can mean leaving someone out because they are different. It might mean not picking them for a game of football.

It might mean leaving them to sit on their own at lunch time.

How would you feel if you were left out?

Racism can mean taking a person's things. It might mean stealing their money. It might mean spoiling their belongings.

Racism can also mean hurting a person. The racists might push or shove them. They might hit them or trip them up.

Both children and adults can be racist.
Children may see or hear their parents
or other adults being racist, and copy them.

But it doesn't matter who is being racist.
Racism is always wrong. It is never okay
for anyone to say or do racist things.

Racism makes people unhappy. It can make them feel unsafe and upset. It can make them scared to go to school or to leave their house.

Racism can make people feel ashamed of who they are, what they look like and where they come from.

What makes you upset?

Why are some people racist? They may think that it's clever to be mean. They may think that they will be more popular if they say racist things.

It may be that they feel afraid of people who are different.

Often, racists don't even know the person they are being mean to. They don't take time to find out anything about them.

They might think that people are strange because they sometimes wear different clothes. They do not understand that this is often a sign of their religion.

In some schools, children come from lots of different countries. Some left their homes because their lives were in danger. Some lost their families.

But other children may not take time getting to know them. They may think that they're stupid because they don't speak English very well.

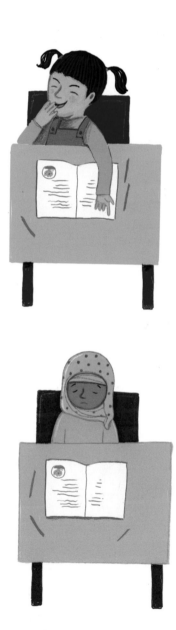

If someone is racist to you, don't keep it to yourself. Tell your parents, teacher or another adult you trust.

Your parents or family could come into school to talk to your class. This could help other children to understand things better.

Who would you tell?

Everyone is different, and that is a very good thing. Imagine how boring life would be if everyone was exactly the same.

We can learn a lot from each other. We can learn about different countries, different religions and different ways of life. We can learn to live together, peacefully and happily.

Notes for parents and teachers

This book can be a useful way for families and professionals to begin a discussion with children about aspects of racism and discrimination. Racism can happen in all walks of life, and has a devastating impact on its victims. In an increasingly multicultural society, it is vital that children learn to tolerate and respect others, and to value difference.

Speaking out about racism can be very daunting, and takes a great deal of courage. Racism is a form of bullying, and victims are often intimidated by the bullies, and afraid to speak out. By identifying someone they can trust and talk to safely – an adult, friend, or an organisation –children can take the first step to being listened to, and finding help.

Emphasising the need for respect and tolerance of others can help to tackle racist attitudes before they become entrenched. Likewise, a discussion of difference and diversity can help children to understand and accept that we are not all the same, and should be valued for the unique human beings that we are. Activities that focus on the above with a class or group will help to reinforce the existing anti-bullying policy in school.

Classroom or group activities:

1. In a carefully managed activity, get the class to think about what it feels like to be discriminated against. For example, treat some of the children - perhaps those with brown hair - more favourably than the others. How do the other children feel? Is it fair that they are treated less favourably because their hair is a different colour?

2. Ask the children what they would do if they saw or heard someone being racist, either to themselves or to a friend. Think about what they would do — keep calm and walk away — and who they would tell — an adult. Talk about how the school has strict rules about racism.

3. Get the group to think about their own families, and to draw a family tree, showing where different family members were born and where they live. This may help to show that most of us have relatives who come from all over the world.

4. Ignorance is often at the root of racism. If possible, and appropriate, you could invite a parent or carer into school to talk to the class about their culture and religion so that misunderstandings can be avoided. Again, if appropriate, the children could prepare questions to ask.

Further Information

Books

Children in Our World: Racism and Intolerance by Louise Spilsbury and Hanane Kai (Wayland, 2018)

Dealing with: Racism by Jane Lacey and Venetia Dean (Franklin Watts, 2017)

The Skin I'm In : A First Look at Racism by Pat Thomas and Lesley Harker (Wayland, 2004)

Websites

bullying.co.uk – Contains advice for parents on what to do about racist bullying

childline.org.uk – Organisation that offers free advice to children under 19

racismnoway.com.au – Anti-racism education rescources for schools

Every effort has been made by the Publishers to ensure that the websites in this book are suitable for children, that they are of the highest educational value, and that they contain no inappropriate or offensive material. However, because of the nature of the Internet, it is impossible to guarantee that the contents of these sites will not be altered. We strongly advise that Internet access is supervised by a responsible adult.